I0473926

Hazard Communication Guidelines for Compliance

U.S. Department of Labor
Alexis M. Herman, Secretary

Occupational Safety and Health Administration
Charles N. Jeffress, Assistant Secretary

OSHA 3111
2000 (Reprinted)

Contents

OSHA's Hazard Communication Standard (HCS) is based on a simple concept—that employees have both a need and a right to know the hazards and identities of the chemicals they are exposed to when working. They also need to know what protective measures are available to prevent adverse effects from occurring. OSHA designed the HCS to provide employees with the information they need to know.

Knowledge acquired under the HCS will help employers provide safer workplaces for their employees. When employees have information about the chemicals being used, they can take steps to reduce exposures, substitute less hazardous materials, and establish proper work practices. These efforts will help prevent the occurrence of work-related illnesses and injuries caused by chemicals.

The HCS addresses the issues of evaluating and communicating chemical hazard information to workers. Evaluation of chemical hazards involves a number of technical concepts, and is a process that requires the professional judgment of experienced experts. That's why the HCS is designed so that employers who simply use chemicals—rather than produce or import them—are not required to evaluate the hazards of those chemicals. Hazard determination is the responsibility of the manufacturers and importers of the chemicals, who then must provide the hazard information to employers that purchase their products

Employers that do not produce or import chemicals need only focus on those parts of the rule that deal with establishing a workplace program and communicating information to their workers. This publication is a general guide for such employers to help them determine what the HCS requires. It does not supplant or substitute for the regulatory provisions, but rather provides a simplified outline of the steps an average employer would follow to meet those requirements.

OSHA has provided a simple summary of the HCS in a pamphlet entitled *Chemical Hazard Communication (OSHA 3084).* Some employers prefer to familiarize themselves with the rule's requirements by reading this pamphlet. A single, free copy may be obtained from your local OSHA Area Office, or by contacting the OSHA Publications Office at (202) 693-1888.

The standard itself is long and some parts are technical, but the basic concepts are simple. In fact, the requirements reflect what many employers have been doing for years. You may find that you already largely comply with many of the provisions and will simply have to modify your existing programs somewhat. If you are operating in an OSHA-approved State Plan State, you must comply with the State's requirements, which may be different than those of the Federal rule. Many of the State Plan States had hazard communication or "right-to-know" laws prior to promulgation of the federal rule. Employers in State Plan States should contact their State OSHA Offices for more information regarding applicable requirements. (See the list of contacts in "States with Approved Plans" at the back of this booklet.)

The HCS requires information to be prepared and transmitted regarding all hazardous chemicals. The HCS covers both physical hazards (such as flammability) and health hazards (such as irritation, lung damage, and cancer.) Most chemicals used in the workplace have some hazard potential, and thus will be covered by the rule.

One difference between this rule and many others adopted by OSHA is that this one is performance-oriented. That means you have the flexibility to adapt the rule to the needs of your workplace, rather than having to follow specific rigid requirements. It also means that you have to exercise more judgment to implement an appropriate and effective program.

The standard's design is simple. Chemical manufacturers and importers must evaluate the hazards of the chemicals they produce or import. Using that information, they must then prepare labels for containers and more detailed technical bulletins called material safety data sheets (MSDSs).

Chemical manufacturers, importers, and distributors of hazardous chemicals are all required to provide the appropriate labels and material safety data sheets to the employers to whom they ship the chemicals. The information must be provided automatically. Every container of hazardous chemicals you receive must be labeled, tagged, or marked with the required information. Your suppliers also must send you a properly completed MSDS at the time of the first shipment of the chemicals, and with the next shipment after the MSDS is updated with new and significant information about the hazards.

You can rely on the information received from your suppliers. You have no independent duty to analyze the chemical or evaluate the hazards of it.

Employers that "use" hazardous chemicals must have a program to ensure the information is provided to exposed employees. "Use" means to package, handle, react, or transfer. This is an intentionally broad scope, and includes any situation where a chemical is present in such a way that employees may be exposed under normal conditions of use or in a foreseeable emergency.

The requirements of the rule that deal specifically with the hazard communication program are found in the standard in paragraphs (e), written hazard communication programs; (f), labels and other forms of warning; (g), material safety data sheets; and (h), employee information and training. The requirements of these paragraphs should be the focus of your attention. Concentrate on becoming familiar with them, using paragraphs (b), scope and application, and (c), definitions, as references when needed to help explain the provisions.

There are two types of work operations where coverage of the rule is limited. These are laboratories and operations where chemicals are only handled in sealed containers (e.g., a warehouse). The limited provisions for these workplaces can be found in paragraph (b), scope and application. Basically, employers having these types of work operations need only keep labels on containers as they are received, maintain material safety data sheets that are received and give employees access to them, and provide information and training for employees. Employers do not have to have written hazard communication programs and lists of chemicals for these types of operations.

The limited coverage of laboratories and sealed container operations addresses the obligation of an employer to the workers in the operations involved, and does not affect the employer's duties as a distributor of chemicals. For example, a distributor may have warehouse operations where employees would be protected under the limited sealed container provisions. In this situation, requirements for obtaining and maintaining MSDSs are limited to providing access to those received with containers while the substance is in the workplace, and requesting MSDSs when employees request access for those not received with the containers. However, as a distributor of hazardous chemicals, that employer will still have responsibility for providing MSDSs to downstream customers at the time of the first shipment and when the MSDS is updated. Therefore, although they may not be required for the employees in the work operation, the distributor may, nevertheless, have to have MSDSs to satisfy other requirements of the rule.

Hazard communication will be a continuing program in your facility. Compliance with HCS is not a "one shot deal." In order to have a successful program, you must assign responsibility for both the initial and ongoing activities that have to be undertaken to comply with the rule. In some cases, these activities may be part of current job assignments. For example, Site Supervisors are frequently responsible for on-the-job training sessions. Early identification of the responsible employees and their involvement in developing your action plan will result in a more effective program design. Involving affected employees also will enhance the evaluation of the effectiveness of your program.

For any safety and health program, success depends on commitment at every level of the organization. This is particularly true for hazard communication, where success requires a change in behavior. This will occur only if employers understand the program and are committed to its success, and if the people presenting the information motivate employees.

The standard requires a list of hazardous chemicals in the workplace as part of the written hazard communication program. The list will eventually serve as an inventory of everything for which you must maintain an MSDS. At this point, however, preparing the list will help you complete the rest of the program since it will give you some idea of the scope of the program required for compliance in your facility.

The best way to prepare a comprehensive list is to survey the workplace. Purchasing records also may help, and certainly employers should establish procedures to ensure that in the future purchasing procedures result in MSDSs being received before using a material in the workplace.

The broadest possible perspective should be taken when doing the survey. Sometimes people think of "chemicals" as being only liquids in containers. The HCS covers chemicals in all physical forms—liquids, solids, gases, vapors, fumes, and mists—whether they are "contained" or not. The hazardous nature of the chemical and the potential for exposure are the factors that determine whether a chemical is covered. If it's not hazardous, it's not covered. If there is no potential for exposure, (e.g., the chemical is inextricably bound and cannot be released), the rule does not cover the chemical.

Look around. Identify the chemicals in containers, including pipes, but also think about chemicals generated in the work operations. For example, welding fumes, dusts, and exhaust fumes are all sources of chemical exposures. Read labels provided by the suppliers on hazard information. Make a list of all chemicals in the workplace that are potentially hazardous. For your own information and planning, you also may want to note on the list the location(s) of the products within the workplace, and an indication of the hazards as found on the label. This will help you as you prepare the rest of your program.

Paragraph (b), scope and application, includes exemptions for various chemicals or workplace situations. After compiling the complete list of chemicals, you should review paragraph (b) to determine if any of the items can be eliminated from the list because they are exempted materials. For example, food, drugs, and cosmetics brought into the workplace for employee consumption are exempt; rubbing alcohol in the first aid kit would not be covered.

Once you have compiled as complete a list as possible of the potentially hazardous chemicals in the workplace, the next step is to determine if you have received material safety data sheets for all of them. Check your files against the inventory you have just compiled. If any are missing, contact your supplier and request one. It is a good idea to document these requests, either by copy of a letter or a note regarding telephone conversations. If you have MSDSs for chemicals that are not on your list, figure out why. Maybe you don't use the chemical anymore. Or maybe you missed it in your survey. Some suppliers do provide MSDSs for products that are not hazardous. These do not have to be maintained by you. If you have questions regarding the hazard status of a chemical, contact the manufacturer, distributor, or importer.

You should not allow employees to use any chemicals for which you have not received an MSDS. The MSDS provides information you need to ensure you have implemented proper protective measures for exposure.

The HCS requires all workplaces where employees are exposed to hazardous chemicals to have a written plan that describes how that facility will implement the standard. Preparation of the plan is not just a paper exercise—all of the elements must be implemented in the workplace to comply with the rule. See paragraph (e) of the standard for the specific requirements regarding written hazard communication programs. The only work operations that do not have to comply with the written plan requirements are laboratories and work operations where employees only handle chemicals in sealed containers. See paragraph (b), scope and application, for the specific requirements for these two types of workplaces.

The plan does not have to be lengthy or complicated. It is intended to be a blueprint for implementing your program—an assurance that all aspects of the requirements have been addressed.

Many trade associations and other professional groups have provided sample programs and other assistance materials to affect employers. These have been very helpful to many employers since they tend to be tailored to the particular industry involved. You may wish to investigate whether your industry trade groups have developed such materials.

Although such general guidance may be helpful, you must remember that the written program has to reflect what you are doing in your workplace. Therefore, if you use a generic program, you must adapt it to address the facility it covers.

For example, the written plan must list the chemicals present at the site and indicate where written materials will be made available to employees. It also may indicate who is responsible for the various aspects of the program in your facility.

If OSHA inspects your workplace for compliance with the HCS, the OSHA compliance officer will ask to see your written plan at the outset of the inspection. In general, the following items will be considered in evaluating your program.

The written program must describe how the requirements for labels and other forms of warning, materials safety data sheets, and employee information and training, are going to be met in your facility. The following discussion provides the type of information compliance officers will be looking for to decide whether you have properly addressed these elements of the hazard communication program.

Labels and Other Forms of Warning

In-plant containers of hazardous chemicals must be labeled, tagged, or marked with the identity of the material and appropriate hazard warnings. Chemical manufacturers, importers, and distributors must ensure that every container of hazardous chemicals they ship is appropriately labeled with such information and with the name and address of the producer or other responsible party. Employers purchasing chemicals can rely on the labels provided by their suppliers. If the material is subsequently transferred by the employer from a labeled container to another container, the employer will have to label that container, unless it is subject to the portable container exemption. See paragraph (f) for specific labeling requirements.

The primary information to be obtained from an OSHA-required label is the identity for the material and appropriate hazard warnings. The identity is any term which appears on the label, the MSDS, and the list of chemicals, and thus links these three sources of information. The identity used by the supplier may be a common or trade name ("Black Magic Formula"), or a chemical name (1, 1, 1 - trichloroethane). The hazard warning is a brief statement of the hazardous effects of the chemical ("flammable," "causes lung damage"). Labels frequently contain other information, such as precautionary measures ("do not use near open flame") but this information is provided voluntarily and is not required by the rule. Labels must be legible and prominently displayed. There are no specific requirements for size or color or any specified test.

With these requirements in mind, the compliance officer will be looking for the following types of information to ensure that labeling is properly implemented in your facility:

- Designation of person(s) responsible for ensuring labeling of in-plant containers;
- Designation of person(s) responsible for ensuring labeling of any shipped container;
- Description of labeling system(s) used;
- Description of written alternatives to labeling of in-plant containers (if used); and,
- Procedures to review and update label information when necessary.

Employers that are purchasing and using hazardous chemicals—rather than producing or distributing them—will primarily be concerned with ensuring that every purchased container is labeled. If materials are transferred into other containers, the employer must ensure that these are labeled as well, unless they fall under the portable container exemption (paragraph f(7)). In terms of labeling systems, you can choose to use the labels provided by your suppliers on the containers. These will generally be verbal text labels, and do not usually include numerical rating systems or symbols that require special training. The most important thing to remember is that this is a continuing duty—all in-plant containers of hazardous chemicals must always be labeled. Therefore, it is important to designate someone to be responsible for ensuring that the labels are maintained as required on the containers in your facility and that newly purchased materials are checked for labels prior to use.

Material Safety Data Sheets

Chemical manufacturers and importers are required to obtain or develop a material safety data sheet for each hazardous chemical they produce or import. Distributors are responsible for ensuring that their customers are provided a copy of these MSDSs. Employers must have an MSDS for each hazardous chemical which they use. Employers may rely on the information received from their suppliers. The specific requirements for material safety data sheets are in paragraph (g) of the standard.

There is no specific format for the MSDS under the rule, although there are specific information requirements. OSHA has developed a nonmandatory format, OSHA Form 174, which may be used by chemical manufacturers and importers to comply with the rule. The MSDS must be in English. You are entitled to receive from your supplier a data sheet which includes all of the information required under the rule. If you do not receive one automatically, you should request one. If you receive one that is obviously inadequate, with, for example, blank spaces that are not completed, you should request an appropriately completed one. If your request for a data sheet or for a corrected data sheet does not produce the information needed, you should contact your local OSHA Area Office for assistance in obtaining the MSDS.

Under the rule, the role of MSDSs is to provide detailed information on each hazardous chemical, including its potential hazardous effects, its physical and chemical characteristics, and recommendations for appropriate protective measures. This information should be useful to you as the employer responsible for designing protective programs, as well as to the workers. If you are not familiar with material safety data sheets and with chemical terminology, you may need to learn to use them yourself. A glossary of MSDS terms may be helpful in this regard. Generally speaking, most employers using hazardous chemicals will primarily be concerned with MSDS information regarding hazardous effects and recommended protective measures. Focus on the sections of the MSDS that are applicable to your situation.

MSDSs must be readily accessible to employees when they are in their work areas during their workshifts. This may be accomplished in many different ways. You must decide what is appropriate for your particular workplace. Some employers keep the MSDSs in a binder in a central location (e.g., in the pickup truck on a construction site.) Others, particularly in workplaces with large numbers of chemicals, computerize the information and provide access through terminals. As long as employees can get the information when they need it, any approach may be used. The employees must have access to the MSDSs themselves—simply having a system where the information can be read to them over the phone is permitted only under the mobile worksite provision, paragraph (g)(9), when employees must travel between workplaces during the shift. In this situation, they have access to the MSDSs prior to leaving the primary worksite, and when they return, so the telephone system is simply an emergency arrangement.

In order to ensure that you have a current MSDS for each chemical in the plant as required, and that you provide employee access, the compliance officers will be looking for the following types of information in your written program:

- Designation of person(s) responsible for obtaining and maintaining the MSDSs;
- How such sheets are to be maintained in the workplace (e.g., in notebooks in the work area(s) or in a computer with terminal access), and how employees can obtain access to them when they are in their work area during the workshift;

- Procedures to follow when the MSDS is not received at the time of the first shipment;
- For producers, procedures to update the MSDS when new and significant health information is found; and,
- Description of alternatives to actual data sheets in the workplace, if used.

For employers using hazardous chemicals, the most important aspect of the written program in terms of MSDSs is to ensure that someone is responsible for obtaining and maintaining the MSDSs for every hazardous chemical in the workplace. The list of hazardous chemicals required to be maintained as part of the written program will serve as an inventory. As new chemicals are purchased, the list should be updated. Many companies have found it convenient to include on their purchase order the name and address of the person designated in their company to receive MSDSs.

Employee Information and Training

Each employee who may be "exposed" to hazardous chemicals when working must be provided information and be trained prior to initial assignment to work with a hazardous chemical, and whenever the hazard changes. "Exposure" or "exposed" under the rule means that an employee is subjected to a hazardous chemical in the course of employment through any route of entry (inhalation, ingestion, skin contact, or absorption) and includes potential (e.g., accidental or possible) exposure. See paragraph (h) of the standard for specific requirements. Information and training may be done either by individual chemical, or by categories of hazards (such as flammability or carcinogenicity). If there are only a few chemicals in the workplace, then you may want to discuss each one individually. Where there are a large number of chemicals, or the chemicals change frequently, you will probably want to train generally based on the hazard categories (e.g., flammable liquids, corrosive materials, carcinogens). Employees will have access to the substance-specific information on the labels and MSDSs. Employers must ensure, however, that employees are made aware of which hazard category a chemical falls within.

Information and training are a critical part of the hazard communication program. Workers obtain information regarding hazards and protective measures through written labels and material safety data sheets. It is through effective information and training, however, that workers will learn to read and understand such information, determine how to acquire and use it in their own workplace, and understand the risks of exposure to the chemical in their workplaces as well as the ways to protect themselves. A properly conducted training program will ensure comprehension and understanding. It is not sufficient to either just read material to the workers or simply hand them material to read. You want to create a climate where workers feel free to ask questions. This will help you to ensure that the information is understood. You must always remember that the underlying purpose of the HCS is to reduce the incidence of chemical source illnesses and injuries. This will be accomplished by modifying behavior through the provision of hazard information and information about protective measures. If your program works, you and your workers will better understand the chemical hazards within the workplace. The procedures you establish, regarding, for example, purchasing, storage, and handling of these chemicals will improve, and thereby reduce the risks posed to employees exposed to the chemical hazards involved. Furthermore, your workers' comprehension also will be increased, and proper work practices will be followed in your workplace.

If you are going to do the training yourself, you will have to understand the material and be prepared to motivate the workers to learn. This is not always an easy task, but the benefits are worth the effort. More information regarding appropriate training can be found in *Training Requirements in OSHA Standards and Training Guidelines (OSHA 2254)*, which contains voluntary training guidelines prepared by OSHA's Training Institute. A copy of this document is available from the Superintendent of Documents, Government Printing Office, P.O. Box 371954, Pittsburgh, PA 15250-7954; (202) 512-1800.

When reviewing your written program regarding information and training, consider the following items:

- Designation of person(s) responsible for conducting training;
- Format of the program used (audiovisuals, class room instruction);
- Elements of the training programs (should be consistent with the elements in paragraph (h) of the HCS); and,

- Procedure to train new employees at the time of their initial assignment to work with a hazardous chemical, and to train employees when introducing a new hazard into the workplace.

The written program should provide enough details about the employer's plans in this area to assess whether or not a good faith effort is being made to train employees. OSHA does not expect that every workers will be able to recite all the information about each chemical in the workplace. In general, the most important aspects of training under the HCS are to ensure that employees are aware that they are exposed to hazardous chemicals, that they know how to read and use labels and material safety data sheets, and that, as a consequence of learning this information, they are following the appropriate protective measures established by the employer. OSHA compliance officers will be talking to employees to determine if they have received training, if they know they are exposed to hazardous chemicals, and if they know where to obtain substance specific information on labels and MSDSs.

The rule does not require employers to maintain records of employee training, but many employers choose to do so. This may help you monitor your own program to ensure that you have trained all employees appropriately. If you already have a training program, you may simply have to supplement it with whatever additional information is required under the HCS. For example, construction employers that are already in compliance with the construction training standard (29 CFR 1926.21) will have little extra training to do.

An employer can provide employees information and training through whatever means found appropriate and protective. Although there would always have to be some training on site (such as informing employees of the location and availability of the written program and MSDSs), employee training may be satisfied in part by general training about the requirements of the HCS which is provided by, for example, trade associations, unions, colleges, and professional schools. In addition, previous training, education, and experience of a worker may relieve the employer of some of the burdens of information and training that worker. Regardless of the method relied upon, however, the employer is always ultimately responsible for ensuring that employees are adequately trained. If the compliance officer finds that the training is deficient, the employer will be cited for the deficiency regardless of who actually provided the training on behalf of the employer.

In addition to these specific items, compliance officers also will be asking the following questions in assessing the adequacy of the program:

- Does a list of the hazardous chemicals exist in each work area or at a central location?
- Are methods the employer will use to inform employees of the hazards of non-routine tasks outlined?
- Are employees informed of the hazards associated with chemicals contained in unlabeled pipes in their work areas?
- On multi-employer worksites, has the employer provided other employers with information about labeling systems and precautionary measures where the other employers have employees exposed to the initial employer's chemicals?
- Is the written program made available to employees and their designated representatives?

If your program adequately addresses the means of communicating information to employees in your workplace and provides answers to the basic questions outlined above, it will comply with the rule.

The following checklist will help to ensure you comply with the rule:

- Obtained a copy of the rule.
- Read and understood the requirements.
- Assigned responsibility for tasks.
- Prepared an inventory of chemicals.
- Ensured containers are labeled.
- Obtained MSDS for each chemical.
- Prepared written program.
- Made MSDSs available to workers.
- Conducted training of workers.
- Established procedures to maintain current program.
- Established procedures to evaluate effectiveness.

If you have a question regarding compliance with HCS, you should contact your local OSHA Area Office for assistance. In addition, each OSHA Regional Office has a Hazard Communication Coordinator who can answer your questions. Free consultation services also are available to assist employers, and information regarding these services can be obtained through the OSHA Area and Regional Offices as well (see lists at the end of this booklet).

Safety and Health Program Management

Effective management of worker safety and health protection is a decisive factor in reducing the extent and severity of work-related injuries and illnesses and their related costs. To assist employers and employees in developing effective safety and health programs, OSHA published recommended *Safety and Health Program Management Guidelines (Federal Register* 54(18):3908-3916, January 26, 1989). These voluntary guidelines apply to all places of employment covered by OSHA.

The guidelines identify four general elements that are critical to the development of a successful safety and health management program:

- management commitment and employee involvement;
- worksite analysis;
- hazard prevention and control; and
- safety and health training.

The guidelines recommend specific actions under each of these general elements to achieve an effective safety and health program. A single, free copy of the guidelines can be obtained from the U.S. Department of Labor, OSHA Publications, P.O. Box 37535, Washington, DC 20013-7535, by sending a self-addressed mailing label with your request.

State Programs

The Occupational Safety and Health Act of 1970 encourages states to develop and operate their own job safety and health plans. States with plans approved under section 18(b) of the OSH Act must adopt standards and enforce requirements that are at least as effective as federal requirements. There are currently 25 state plan states: 23 of these states administer plans covering both private and public (state and local public government) employees; the other two states, Connecticut and New York, cover public employees only. Plan states must adopt standards comparable to federal requirements within six months of a federal standard's promulgation. Until such time as a state standard is promulgated, Federal OSHA provides interim enforcement assistance, as appropriate, in these states. A listing of approved state plans appear at the end of this publication.

Consultation Services

Consultation assistance is available on request to employers who want help in establishing and maintaining a safe and healthful workplace. Largely funded by OSHA, the service is provided at no cost to the employer. Primarily developed for smaller employers with more hazardous operations, the consultation service is delivered by state government agencies or universities employing professional safety consultants and health consultants. Comprehensive assistance includes an appraisal of all work practices and environmental hazards of the workplace and all aspects of the employer's present job safety and health program.

The program is separate from OSHA's inspection efforts. No penalties are proposed or citations issued for any safety or health problems identified by the consultant. The service is confidential.

For more information concerning consultation assistance, see the list of consultation projects at the end of this publication.

Voluntary Protection Programs (VPP)

Voluntary Protection Programs (VPP) and onsite consultation services, when coupled with an effective enforcement program, expand worker protection to help meet the goals of the OSH Act. The three VPPs—Star, Merit, and Demonstration—are designed to recognize outstanding achievement by companies that have success-fully incorporated comprehensive safety and health programs into their total management system. They motivate others to achieve excellent safety and health results in the same outstanding way as they establish a cooperative relationship among employers, employ-ees, and OSHA.

For additional information on VPP and how to apply, contact your nearest OSHA area or regional office listed at the end of this publication.

Training and Education

OSHA Area Offices offer a variety of information services, such as publications, audiovisual aids, technical advice, and speakers for special engagements. The OSHA Training Institute in Des Plaines,

IL, provides basic and advanced courses in safety and health for federal and state compliance officers, state consultants, federal agency personnel, and private sector employers, employees, and their representatives.

OSHA also provides funds to nonprofit organizations, through grants to conduct workplace training and education in subjects where OSHA believes there is a lack of workplace training. Grants are awarded annually and grant recipients arc expected to contribute 20 percent of the total grant cost.

For more information on grants, training, and education, contact the OSHA Training Institute, Office of Training and Education, 1555 Times Drive, Des Plaines, IL 60018, (847) 297-4810; (847) 297-4874 fax.

Electronic Information

Internet-OSHA standards, interpretations, directives, and additional information are now on the World Wide Web at http://www.osha.gov/ and http://www.osha-slc.gov/.

CD-ROM—A wide variety of OSHA materials, including standards, interpretations, directives, and more can be purchased on CD-ROM from the U.S. Government Printing Office. To order, write to the Superintendent of Documents, P.O. Box 371954, Pittsburgh, PA 15250-7954, or phone (202) 512-1800. Specify OSHA Regulations, Documents, and Technical Information on CD-ROM (ORDT), GPO Order NO. S/N 729-013-00000-5. The price is $48 per year ($57.50 foreign); $17 per single copy ($21.25 foreign).

Emergencies

For life-threatening situations, call (800) 32 1 -OSHA. Complaints will go immediately to the nearest OSHA area or state office for help.

For further information on any OSHA program, contact your nearest OSHA area or regional office listed at the end of this publication.

Single free copies of the following publications can be obtained from the OSHA Publications Office, P.0. Box 37535, Washington, DC 20013-7535. Send a self-addressed mailing label with your request.

All About OSHA – OSHA 2056

Chemical Hazard Communication – OSHA 3084

Consultation Services for the Employer – OSHA 3074

Employee Workplace Rights – OSHA 3021

Employer Rights and Responsibilities Following an OSHA Inspection – OSHA 3000

How to Prepare for Workplace Emergencies – OSHA 3088

OSHA Inspections – OSHA 2098

Personal Protective Equipment – OSHA 3077

Respiratory Protection – OSHA 3079

The following publications may be ordered at cost, from the Superintendent of Documents, U.S. Government Printing Office, Washington DC 20402, (202) 512-1800. Include GPO Order No. and make checks payable to Superintendent of Documents.

Code of Federal Regulations – Title 29, Part 1926

Construction (OSHA) ($30)
Order No. S/N 869-038-00107-1

OSHA Safety and Health Standards (29 CFR 1910.1000 to End)
($28) Order No. S/N 869-038-00105-5.

Handbook for Small Business – OSHA 2209 ($7.50)
Order No. 029-016-00176-0.

Commissioner
Alaska Department of Labor
1111 West 8th Street
Room 304
Juneau, AK 99801-1149
(907) 465-2700

Director
Industrial Commission of Arizona
800 W. Washington
Phoenix, AZ 85007-2922
(602) 542-5795

Director
California Department
  of Industrial Relations
455 Golden Gate Avenue -
  10th Floor
San Francisco, CA 94102
(415) 703-5050

Commissioner
Connecticut Department of Labor
200 Folly Brook Boulevard
Wethersfield, CT 06109
(860) 566-5123

Director
Hawaii Department of Labor
  and Industrial Relations
830 Punchbowl Street
Honolulu, HI 96813
(808) 586-8844

Commissioner
Indiana Department of Labor
  State Office Building
402 West Washington Street
Room W195
Indianapolis, IN 46204-2751
(317) 232-2378

Commissioner
Iowa Division of Labor Services
1000 E. Grand Avenue
Des Moines, IA 50319-0209
(515) 281-3447

Secretary
Kentucky Labor Cabinet
1047 U.S. Highway, 127 South,
  Suite 4
Frankfort, KY 40601
(502) 564-3070

Commissioner
Maryland Division of Labor
  and Industry
Department of Labor, Licensing,
  and Regulation
1100 N. Eutaw Street,
Room 613
Baltimore, MD 21201-2206
(410) 767-2215

Director
Michigan Department
   of Consumer and Industry
   Services
P.O. Box 30643
Lansing, MI 48909-8143
(517) 322-1814

Commissioner
Minnesota Department of Labor
   and Industry
443 Lafayette Road
St. Paul, MN 55155-4307
(651) 296-2342

Administrator
Nevada Division of Industrial
   Relations
400 West King Street
Carson City, NV 89710
(775) 687-3032

Secretary
New Mexico Environment
   Department
1190 St. Francis Drive
P.O. Box 26110
Santa Fe, NM 87502
(505) 827-2850

Commissioner
New York Department of Labor
W. Averell Harriman State Office
   Building - 12, Room 500
Albany, NY 12240
(518) 457-2741

Commissioner
North Carolina Department
   of Labor
4 West Edenton Street
Raleigh, NC 27601-1092
(919) 807-7166

Administrator
Department of Consumer
   and Business Services
Occupational Safety and Health
   Division (OR-OSHA)
350 Winter Street, NE,
   Room 430
Salem, OR 97310-0220
(503) 378-3272

Secretary
Puerto Rico Department
   of Labor and Human Resources
Prudencio Rivera Martinez
   Building
505 Munoz Rivera Avenue
Hato Rey, PR 00918
(787) 754-2119

Director
South Carolina Department
  of Labor, Licensing, and
  Regulation
Koger Office Park,
  Kingstree Building
110 Centerview Drive
P.O. Box 11329
Columbia, SC 29210
(803) 896-4300

Commissioner
Tennessee Department of Labor
Attention: Robert Taylor
710 James Robertson Parkway
Nashville, TN 37243-0659
(615) 741-2582

Commissioner
Labor Commission of Utah
160 East 300 South, 3rd Floor
P.O. Box 146650
Salt Lake City, UT 84114-6650
(801) 530-6898

Commissioner
Vermont Department
  of Labor and Industry
National Life Building -
  Drawer 20
National Life Drive
Montpelier, VT 05620-3401
(802) 828-5098

Commissioner
Virginia Department of Labor
  and Industry
Powers-Taylor Building
13 South 13th Street
Richmond, VA 23219
(804) 786-2377

Commissioner
Virgin Islands Department
  of Labor
2203 Church Street
Christiansted
St. Croix, VI 00820-4660
(340) 773-1994

Director
Washington Department
  of Labor and Industries
P.O. Box 44001
Olympia, WA 98504-4001
(360) 902-4200

Administrator
Worker's Safety and
  Compensation Division (WSC)
Wyoming Department
  of Employment
Herschler Building,
  2nd Floor East
122 West 25th Street
Cheyenne, WY 82002
(307) 777-7786

State	Telephone
Alabama	(205) 348-3033
Alaska	(907) 269-4957
Arizona	(602) 542-1695
Arkansas	(501) 682-4522
California	(415) 703-5270
Colorado	(970) 491-6151
Connecticut	(860) 566-4550
Delaware	(302) 761-8219
District of Columbia	(202) 576-6339
Florida	(850) 922-8955
Georgia	(404) 894-2643
Guam	011(671) 475-0136
Hawaii	(808) 586-9100
Idaho	(208) 426-3283
Illinois	(312) 814-2337
Indiana	(317) 232-2688
Iowa	(515) 281-7162
Kansas	(785) 296-7476
Kentucky	(502) 564-6895
Louisiana	(504) 342-9601
Maine	(207) 624-6460
Maryland	(410) 880-4970
Massachusetts	(617) 727-3982
Michigan	(517) 322-6823(H)
	(517) 322-1809(S)
Minnesota	(612) 297-2393
Mississippi	(601) 987-3981
Missouri	(573) 751-3403
Montana	(406) 444-6418
Nebraska	(402) 471-4717
Nevada	(702) 486-9140
New Hampshire	(603) 271-2024
New Jersey	(609) 292-3923
New Mexico	(505) 827-4230
New York	(518) 457-2238
North Carolina	(919) 807-2905
North Dakota	(701) 328-5188
Ohio	(614) 644-2246
Oklahoma	(405) 528-1500

Oregon	(503) 378-3272
Pennsylvania	(724) 357-2396
Puerto Rico	(787) 754-2171
Rhode Island	(401) 222-2438
South Carolina	(803) 734-9614
South Dakota	(605) 688-4101
Tennessee	(615) 741-7036
Texas	(512) 804-4640
Utah	(801) 530-6901
Vermont	(802) 828-2765
Virginia	(804) 786-6359
Virgin Islands	(340) 772-1315
Washington	(360) 902-5638
West Virginia	(304) 558-7890
Wisconsin	(608) 266-8579(H)
	(262) 523-3040(S)
Wyoming	(307) 777-7786

(H) - Health
(S) - Safety

Area	Telephone
Albany, NY	(518) 464-4338
Albuquerque, NM	(505) 248-5302
Allentown, PA	(610) 776-0592
Anchorage, AK	(907) 271-5152
Appleton, WI	(920) 734-4521
Austin, TX	(512) 916-5783
Avenel, NJ	(908) 750-3270
Bangor, ME	(207) 941-8179
Baton Rouge, LA	(225) 389-0474
Bayside, NY	(718) 279-9060
Bellevue, WA	(206) 553-7520
Billings, MT	(406) 247-7494
Birmingham, AL	(205) 731-1534
Bismarck, ND	(701) 250-4521
Boise, ID	(208) 321-2960
Bowmansville, NY	(716) 684-3891
Braintree, MA	(617) 565-6924
Bridgeport, CT	(203) 579-5516
Calumet City, IL	(708) 891-3800
Carson City, NV	(702) 885-6963
Charleston, WV	(304) 347-5937
Cincinnati, OH	(513) 841-4132
Cleveland, OH	(216) 522-3818
Columbia, SC	(803) 765-5904
Columbus, OH	(614) 469-5582
Concord, NH	(603) 225-1629
Corpus Christi, TX	(512) 888-3420
Dallas, TX	(214) 320-2400
Denver, CO	(303) 844-5285
Des Plaines, IL	(847) 803-4800
Des Moines, IA	(515) 284-4794
Eau Claire, WI	(715) 832-9019
El Paso, TX	(915) 534-6251
Englewood, CO	(303) 843-4500
Erie, PA	(814) 833-5758
Fairview Heights, IL	(618) 632-8612
Fort Lauderdale, FL	(954) 424-0242
Fort Worth, TX	(817) 428-2470
Frankfort, KY	(502) 227-7024
Guaynabo, PR	(787) 277-1560
Harrisburg, PA	(717) 782-3902
Hartford, CT	(860) 240-3152
Hasbrouck Heights, NJ	(201) 288-1700
Honolulu, HI	(808) 541-2685
Houston, TX	(281) 286-0583

Houston, TX	(281) 591-2438
Indianapolis, IN	(317) 226-7290
Jackson, MS	(601) 965-4606
Jacksonville, FL	(904) 232-2895
Kansas City, MO	(816) 483-9531
Linthicum, MD	(410) 865-2055
Little Rock, AR	(501) 324-6291
Lubbock, TX	(806) 472-7681
Madison, WI	(608) 441-5388
Marlton, NJ	(609) 757-5181
Methuen, MA	(617) 565-8110
Milwaukee, WI	(414) 297-3315
Minneapolis, MN	(612) 664-5460
Mobile, AL	(334) 441-6131
Nashville, TN	(615) 781-5423
New York, NY	(212) 466-2482
Norfolk, VA	(757) 441-3820
North Aurora, IL	(630) 896-8700
Oklahoma City, OK	(405) 231-5351
Omaha, NE	(402) 221-3182
Parsippany, NJ	(201) 263-1003
Peoria, IL	(309) 671-7033
Philadelphia, PA	(215) 597-4955
Phoenix, AZ	(602) 640-2007
Pittsburgh, PA	(412) 395-4903
Portland, ME	(207) 780-3178
Portland, OR	(503) 326-2251
Providence, RI	(401) 528-4663
Raleigh, NC	(919) 856-4770
Sacramento, CA	(916) 566-7470
Salt Lake City, UT	(801) 487-0680
San Diego, CA	(619) 557-2909
Savannah, GA	(912) 652-4393
Smyrna, GA	(770) 984-8700
Springfield, MA	(413) 785-0123
St. Louis, MO	(314) 425-4249
Syracuse, NY	(315) 451-0808
Tampa, FL	(813) 626-1177
Tarrytown, NY	(914) 524-7510
Toledo, OH	(419) 259-7542
Tucker, GA	(770) 493-6644
Westbury, NY	(516) 334-3344
Wichita, KS	(316) 269-6644
Wilkes-Barre, PA	(717) 826-6538
Wilmington, DE	(302) 573-6115

Region I
(CT,* MA, ME, NH, RI, VT*)
JFK Federal Building
Room E-340
Boston, MA 02203
Telephone: (617) 565-9860

Region II
(NJ, NY,* PR,* VI*)
201 Varick Street
Room 670
New York, NY 10014
Telephone: (212) 337-2378

Region III
(DC, DE, MD,* PA, VA,* WV)
The Curtis Center - Suite 740 West
170 S. Independence Mall West
Philadelphia, PA 19106-3309
Telephone: (215) 861-4900

Region IV
(AL, FL, GA, KY,* MS, NC,*
SC,* TN*)
Atlanta Federal Center
61 Forsyth Street, SW, Room 6T50
Atlanta, GA 30303
Telephone: (404) 562-2300

Region V
(IL, IN,* MI,* MN,* OH, WI)
230 South Dearborn Street
Room 3244
Chicago, IL 60604
Telephone: (312) 353-2220

Region VI
(AR, LA, MN,* OK, TX)
525 Griffin Street
Room 602
Dallas, TX 75202
Telephone: (214) 767-4731

Region VII
(IA,* KS, MO, NE)
City Center Square
1100 Main Street, Suite 800
Kansas City, MO 64105
Telephone: (816) 426-5861

Region VIII
(CO, MT, ND, SD, UT,* WY*)
1999 Broadway
Suite 1690
Denver, CO 80802-5716
Telephone: (303) 844-1600

Region IX
(American Samoa, AZ,* CA,*
Guam, HI,* NV,* Trust
Territories of the Pacific)
71 Stevenson Street
4th Floor
San Francisco, CA 94105
Telephone: (415) 975-4310

Region X
(AK,* ID, OR,* WA*)
1111 Third Avenue
Suite 715
Seattle, WA 98101-3212
Telephone: (206) 553-5930

---

*These states and territories operate their own OSHA-approved job safety
and health programs (Connecticut and New York plans cover public employees
only). States with approved programs must have a standard that is identical to,
or at least as effective as, the federal standard.

www.ingramcontent.com/pod-product-compliance
Lightning Source LLC
Chambersburg PA
CBHW071556170526
45166CB00004B/1693